Dear
Little Ones

Book 1

Hope, Help, and Healing for Your Inner Children

Dear
Little Ones

Book 1

Jade Miller
illustrated by Germán Zaninetti

Published by
MultiFaceted
Press

Cover and interior design by Christy Collins,
Constellation Book Design
Illustrated by Germán Zaninetti

ISBN (paperback): 978-1-7369902-0-9
ISBN (ebook): 978-1-7369902-1-6

Printed in the United States of America

Introduction

When I wrote the first *Dear Little Ones* book in 2015, I'd been blogging at *Thoughts From J8* for about a year. I wrote about dissociation, life as a multiple, and recovering from C-PTSD, trauma, ritual abuse, and attachment disorders. Someone in an online forum commented that they wished there were a book written for younger child self-states, and the idea intrigued me. Not too long after that, I wrote *Dear Little Ones Book 1: Hope, Help and Healing for Your Inner Children*.

The response to the book was unexpected. I hoped I would be able to sell enough copies to cover the publishing costs. But there were much bigger things in store for this book.

Within a year, *Dear Little Ones Book 1* had reached an international readership. It appeared on must-read lists of many grassroots trauma survivor networks all over the globe, from the U.S. to the United Kingdom to Australia. Trauma survivors, therapists, family members and friends of survivors were leaving positive reviews and sending emails to tell me how the book had touched them. And it didn't stop there.

Dear Little Ones Book 1 has been an Amazon bestseller numerous times since its original publication, and sales have consistently increased over time, despite my lack of marketing skills. This book has a special kind of magic.

My favorite emails are the ones I get from child self-states, shyly telling me that their therapist or another adult had read the book to them, and thanking me for helping them understand the world better.

I never intended for *Dear Little Ones* to become a series, but I often received emails from readers asking if I could write more books for inner children. So I wrote the second and third books in the series in 2016 and 2018, respectively.

I am thrilled that these books have made a positive difference to so many people's lives. I am even more thrilled that I have been able to create a healing resource for other survivors out of my lived experience of abuse and trauma. My hope for these books is that they reach far and wide and contribute to a generation of people that heals from their trauma and breaks the cycle of pain for generations to come.

L.R. Knost said, "Healing old hurts can only begin when the children we once were feel safe enough to speak their hearts to the adults we are now."

I hope that the *Dear Little Ones* books can help start these conversations.

Dear little ones,

I know things might be scary and confusing right now, but my name is Jade and I'm here to help.

I want to help you understand what's happening, so I wrote this book for you.

I'm friends with a lot of little ones, and I care about them very much.

I care about you, too.

If you have a special stuffed animal or baby doll or a comfy blanket to hold while someone reads this to you, you can go get it if you want. Or ask someone to help you.

Snuggle up and use your best listening ears.

A long time ago, things happened in the outside world that may have been painful or scary or confusing.

Sweet little one, none of those things were your fault.

Other people made bad choices, or may have made choices that made you feel scared or confused, but it had nothing to do with you.

Sometimes when things happen
that children don't understand,
they think it's their fault.

Sometimes children are even told
they are bad, or that bad things
are their fault, but it's not true.
Not even a little bit.

No matter what happened,
no matter what anyone told you,
it was not your fault.

You are wonderful,
you are beautiful,
you are innocent,
and you are valuable.

You have amazing things
inside you, like bravery,
trust, and fun. And you
are very, very smart.

That is the real truth.

You are worthy of being
taken care of and loved
in a safe and healthy way.

People should have protected
you and treasured you.

I'm so sorry they didn't.

But it's not your fault.

It's important for you to know that those bad things are not happening anymore.

You are safe now.

But because of those things that happened, other people needed to be born on the inside in order to help the body stay alive.

Some of those inside people
are older now, because they
kept growing up.

The body is also older now.

Even if you feel little,
your body is grown up.

See how tall you are?

One day, when you are ready,
you can grow up too,
if you want to.
But you don't have to.

You get to choose.

Until then, see if you can get to know the other people on the inside. There may be some people your age on the inside that can be your friends!

You may also find some other people on the inside who can help you and take care of you.

They can be like a big brother or sister, and keep you safe.

They can help you understand things.

Sometimes there are people on the inside who seem kind of scary.

They might be angry or loud or bossy.

Even though they look scary,
they are just trying to help.
They are helping in the only
ways that they know how.

Try to be nice to them even
if they don't seem friendly.
They are hurting and need to
know that they are valuable too.

In time, as people are nice to them,
they will feel better and learn other
ways to help and how to be friends.

Once you start to make friends
on the inside, it's important to
let the older ones have time in
the outside world to find helpers
who can show all of you how
to work together like a team.

This will make things less scary
and confusing—but not all at once.
It will take a lot of time and
a lot of brave choices.

When your big brothers or
big sisters find a helper on
the outside who is safe, ask
them when you can have a
turn to talk to the helper.

You do not have to talk to them
unless you want to. You can watch
for awhile, until you feel ready.

You can choose what feels safe to you.

Being able to make a choice is very important.

You couldn't choose when scary things were happening in the past, but you can choose now.

You have a voice.

Whenever you are ready to
talk to your outside helpers,
try to tell them everything
you're thinking and feeling.

That way, they can help you make
choices that are best for you.

If you feel scared or upset or confused, and you need help, ask one of your inside friends to help you know what to say, or how to talk about it.

Sometimes drawing helps.

If the feelings get too big,
take a break.

Do something that will help
you remember that things
are different now.

Some people like to take walks
so they can get some fresh air.

Some people like to turn on music,
or get a drink or yummy snack.

Do whatever feels best for you until
the feelings are not so big anymore.

Keep trusting your big brothers and sisters on the inside, and keep listening to your helper on the outside.

Things won't always be so scary or confusing.

One day things will be better.

One day, when the time is right,
you'll be ready to choose what
you'd like to do.

Some little ones choose to grow up.

Some little ones choose to go to
a very safe place on the inside
and rest.

Some little ones choose to stay little, and take turns playing and exploring in the outside world.

This is something you get to choose, too.

You can choose whatever feels the best to you.

You always get to choose.

You were never created to be hurt or scared or unloved.

You were created for a life of joy, and fun, and love, where you can dream big dreams and have grand adventures.

Things may be hard for a little while, but as you keep making friends and keep learning how to make good choices, you will feel better and better.

If there are things you don't understand, let your big brothers and sisters on the inside help you.

Everyone on the inside is very, very important.

Everyone on the inside has valuable things to share.

So keep listening to each other and working together.

I wish all and only good things for you as you continue to take steps that will bring you into a life of truth and joy and peace.

I am with you in my heart, and I am cheering for you.

Love, Jade

I'm blowing you a kiss!

About the Author

JADE MILLER was born in east Tennessee. She is a survivor of ritual abuse and human trafficking, peer support worker, trauma recovery support group facilitator and author.

Jade has been writing since she was a young child, illustrating her own stories and winning writing awards in elementary school all the way through high school. She studied writing and editing in college, and made her publishing debut with the first *Dear Little Ones* book in 2015. Two additional *Dear Little Ones* books followed, as well as an ebook on attachment theory. Her books have been translated into several languages and have received international attention and praise from trauma survivors and therapists. She is also working on her first novel and a memoir.

Jade believes that the idea of one single cohesive "personality" is mostly a social construct. She suspects that universal multiplicity is much more likely—the concept that every person is a collection of self-states, and their upbringing and life experiences determine the level of awareness and cooperation between those self-states.

Jade is a peer support worker to people who identify as multiple or plural and/or have

Dissociative Identity Disorder. She also offers education for mental health professionals drawing from her lived experiences and a private social media group for other multiples. Learn more about working with her one on one at www.peersupportformultiples.com. Jade's blog can be found at www.thoughtsfromj8.com.

For more information on the *Dear Little Ones* books, visit www.multifacetedpress.com.

About the Illustrator

GERMÁN ZANINETTI is an illustrator living in Argentina, where he studied for an illustrating career at Escuela de Artes Visuales Martin Malharro. He prefers to work on mythological themes (mostly Greek and Egyptian), but also feels comfortable with child themes. This is his first freelance project.

You can email him at: harryzon88@gmail.com.

Made in the USA
Coppell, TX
22 July 2022